Thieves in the Family

Also by Maria Lisella

Two Naked Feet, Poets Wear Prada (2009)
Amore on Hope Street, Finishing Line Press (2009)

Thieves in the Family

Maria Lisella

The New York Quarterly Foundation, Inc.
New York, New York

NYQ Books™ is an imprint of The New York Quarterly Foundation, Inc.

The New York Quarterly Foundation, Inc.
P. O. Box 2015
Old Chelsea Station
New York, NY 10113

www.nyq.org

Copyright © 2014 by Maria Lisella

All rights reserved. No part of this book may be used or reproduced in any manner whatsoever without written permission of the author except in the case of brief quotations embodied in critical articles and reviews.

First Edition

Set in New Baskerville

Layout by Joseph Hamersly
Cover Design by Raymond P. Hammond
Author Photo by Nancy Ruhling
Cover Illustration: "The Thief of Hearts"; 4" x 5"; mixed media
            by JF Biron, 2012 | www.inkyoursoul.com

Library of Congress Control Number: 2014934953

ISBN: 978-1-935520-72-6

Thieves in the Family

Acknowledgments

My grateful acknowledgment to the editors of the following journals, and anthologies in which poems appearing in this volume were originally published:

Avanti Popolo: Italian Americans Sail Beyond Columbus; Curaggia: An Anthology of Women of Italian Descent, Eco-Logic, Feile-Festa, First Literary Review-East, For Better or Worse: An Anthology of Poetry on Marriage, Fox Chase Review, Future Earth, Gradiva, Italian Americana, LIPS, Liqueur 44 (France), Long Island Sounds, Maintenan 6, Mobius, New Verse News, Newtown Literary, New York Quarterly, North Sea Poetry Scene, Paterson Literary Review, Performance Poets Literary Review, Philadelphia Poets, Pirene's Fountain, Red Wheelbarrow Poets, River Poets Journal, and *Skidrow Penthouse.*

And, thank you to the members of the online poetry circle, Brevitas, the Madison Avenue Poets, in particular, the late Diana Festa, the Italian American Writers Association, and Angelo Verga.

Dedicated to Giovannina whose hands sewed and tailored, ironed and washed, cooked and made all the places I come from...

Contents

I.

Since You Asked   /*15*
The Same   /*16*
For the Love of Bread   /*17*
No Earrings for Tina   /*18*
Polish Interrupted   /*19*
Las Andeanas in Astoria   /*20*
L'americana—The American   /*21*
Soledad—Solitude   /*22*
Immigration   /*23*

II.

Father, fix it, please.   /*27*
La Ciudad de los Muertos—City of the Dead, Havana, 2003   /*28*
The Last Time   /*30*
Dead Rose   /*31*
Salt Stings   /*32*
Just One Thing   /*33*
Romance   /*34*
Signs   /*35*
Wakes   /*36*
I Listen   /*37*

III.

Lovestuck /41
How ever did you know /42
Un Beso en Cuba—A Kiss in Cuba /43
La Nebbia Veneziana—Fog in Venice /44
Birds on a Box /46
Déjà vu /47
Demons /48
Spring /49
When Magritte Wasn't Looking /50
Bats /51

IV.

Skippy /55
A tavola!—Sit Down at the Table! /56
Lethal /57
Marble King /58
Cornrows /60
Inside /62
Thieves in the Family /63
Before It Gets Tough /64
Brother /66
We must have known /67
The Call /68
Empty Chairs /70
Bleach *y chorizos* /71
The Boys /72

V.

Mantras / 75
Sparrow Hawks / 76
Chetty's Cats / 77
Mad with Fear / 78
Just Boys / 79
Illegal / 80
Autumn in the Algarve / 81
Missive from the Sunny Southwest / 82
Hunger / 83

VI.

Goes Silent / 87
Small Victories / 88
Named for Royalty / 89
C'era una volta—Once Upon a Time / 90
Coming Up for Air / 91
Away / 92
Amore on Hope Street / 94
Afraid / 96
Ladies who lunch / 97
Longing / 98
Comfort Zone / 99
My Rain / 100

Thieves in the Family

I.

Since You Asked

I am from dank wine cellars in South Jamaica—from cousins named Johnny, Joey, Nicky, and Frankie who harvested Queens' grapes. I am from a line of women sporting artichoke haircuts and pink collars. I am also from a Carmine Street tenement that lost its address in the last century. I am from the mind of a man who sent other men to the moon—from a red-shingled house that echoed with three languages at once. I am from a bar in Marseilles, a meadow in Molise, but most of all, I am from 116th Drive off Sutphin and Foch Boulevards—a zebra-colored neighborhood where everyone called my grandmother mamma, where cornrows were everywhere, but never in fashion. I am from tomato and basil plants strung low with rainbow-colored yarns leaning sideways in damp summer soil. I am from gnarled hands that sew and tailor, iron and wash, cook and make all the places I come from.

The Same

I want to tell
the little Chinese women
with the loud voices
to sit beside each other
so they don't shout
across the subway car,
over my head,
shattering
my space.
I offer my seat.
The lady with the
short-cropped perm
red as a rooster's comb
in a Chinese market
gives me a toothy grin
the essence of onions, garlic
shakes her head
from side to side like a
tai chi exercise, no, no, no
as if to say, "I may shop in Costco
wear jeans, a North Face down jacket,
but you'll never
make me a Westerner,
won't drop
my Chinese voice
a single decibel
to suit you and your
Anglo-silence on subway cars
as if they were chapels
or private property."
I hear my grandmother's
staccato Calabrese vowels
clang against brick walls
in an alleyway in Queens
with the same defiance,
the same pride,
the same sorrow to be in America.

For the Love of Bread

A loaf of bread
sat on the table
at every meal.
An edge against poverty,
the last call,
the final loss,
the promise
of more
tomorrow.
It could not be
just any bread.
It had to be crusty,
cracked in its center
but not split.
Long, or round,
seed speckled,
yellow inside.
It could not be
a thin slice of
American white bread.
A slice of the old country
had to be handmade,
to have risen twice,
to be bought
at a bakery from
an artisan baker.
Brought back in a
paper sleeve,
never plastic wrapped,
with aromas of chestnut,
and home.

No Earrings for Tina

I was seven when I realized
none of the girls in school wore pierced earrings.

My mother insisted,

said it was *buona fortuna* for girls to start off life with a piece
    of gold in their ears.
She didn't understand this was America,
where only the *zingare* wore gold in their ears and told
    fortunes.
American girls never put holes in their ears.
My father took me to the movies on Saturdays.

When they were sad, I would cry.

Once we saw *Queen Christina* when Greta Garbo laughed
    out loud for the first time in the movies.
She threw her head back and I saw she had no gold earrings
    in her ears and she wasn't even an American.
On the way home we rode the elevated train.
When my father wasn't looking, I unhooked my earrings,
threw them out the window.

Polish Interrupted

Their necks rose with voices
that bellowed at weddings and wakes
with songs from the old country.
From Warsaw and Cracow
they arrived in Greenpoint.
An uninterrupted Polish experience—
walked arm in arm,
men with men, women with women;
ate their kielbasa, pierogies, drank vodka and beer,
danced the polka, held candles at St. Stanislaus vigils.
Now they drive American cars,
wear white-collared shirts.
My friends don't sing anymore;
first they forgot the words, then the melodies.

Las Andeanas in Astoria

They arrive from Ecuador,
Bolivia, Peru, to the sidewalks
of Queens, they step
in sneakers without socks,
bowler hats top
their gold-toned faces,
hair tied back
in little girl braids
that swivel from side to side
between rounded shoulder blades.

They stuff garbage bags
with glass and plastic bottles.
Pile them high above
their heads inside blue clouds
billowing out of shopping carts.

Built low to the ground
like squat mountain climbers,
their bodies are silent.
Cartwheels squeak,
high-pitched notes rattle.
Gray squirrels scatter
in black branches above.
If these women were back home
trudging wheelbarrows
across the *Mita del Mundo* at noon,
they would not cast a shadow.

Half wear their husbands'
work shirts, others,
their teenage sons' t-shirts
down to their knees.

They lift their heads or smile,
a flash of gold from
wide even mouths.

L'americana—The American

The women's talk moves
to women's talk.
"And your clothes, they cannot be
from America.
Real Americans wear
pink and blue
and socks with sandals like Germans."

New York is not *L'America*.
The national color is black there,
but not for mourning,
I try to say.

I don't look like a *real* American,
because I remain a Mediterranean hybrid
with the suspicious heart of a peasant
on both sides of the Atlantic.

Soledad—Solitude

Easy
in a city of 10 million.

Scope a corner seat
on the subway
next to a wall or window.
Hunker down
into the orange curve
that hugs my butt
lean into the synthetic wall
that chills my shoulder.

Rolling onboard with
a cranky baby in a stroller
a Mexican family sits beside me.
The teenager
watches me,
divines the mysteries
of American body language.

I join them.
Eavesdrop on his parents'
Spanish exchange,
note his edgy English responses,
eager to leave them behind.

Immigration

On a one-lane road
I drive through Sicily.

Green groves spiked
with yellow globes
like Christmas ornaments
skinned in summer,
soaked in syrup,
sold from barrels
at roadside stands.

Preserved lemons,
Morgan lemons,
thick-skinned lemons
with salt sprinkled
on the back of my hand
to lick, suck, sip beer.

In the shade of emerald leaves
stick figures
bend, reach, toss lemons
a euro for five kilos
end in a bell jar
on my kitchen counter
in New York City.

II.

Father, fix it, please.

The dark befriends me
here in the basement
in your well-appointed
workshop of Able Steel
shelves, pegboards, bits.

You could fix anything.
TV and radio carcasses
were respected in this room,
not tossed—were instead,
small engineering feats.

You explained
algebra and binary
numbers in this laboratory.
I try never to forget
anything about you.

Sometimes I lose your voice,
but remember the crease in your
starched white sleeve
as you repaired a pen, a frame,
a dining room chair.

La Ciudad de los Muertos—City of the Dead, Havana, 2003

This is the Cadillac of cemeteries,
also called the Necropolis, he says,
Let us talk about the aristocracy.

Pedro—hairless, round,
half-man, half-boy
guides the uninitiated.

They are buried beneath
marble from Carrara, Italy,
France and the quarries of Spain.

Pedro walks the cemetery daily
guiding groups of American travelers
sneaking visits to this soggy Cuban land.

But no matter, the important fact is
they may have been rich, but
now they are very, very dead.

Pablo knows he can impress us
with ghoulish details.
Even dying is complicated on this island.

It takes months for bodies to disintegrate
in Havana: two years for tendons to shrivel,
ossos, bones are boxed, buried again.

Two million rest here, outnumbering
the living at times in Havana, once
Chinese Coolie's plots, then the opulent moved in.

Like a circus barker in the center ring,
One of the world's most luxurious cemeteries—
the others are in Buenos Aires, Paris, Genoa.

We follow Pedro like schoolchildren
under decayed Moorish gateways,
limestone images of faith and hope in Havana.

The Last Time

The last time he rolled over on his side
he slipped off the pillows propping his head
just high enough to breathe as if this tiny altitude
would save him. The rubber oxygen mask,
so like his swimming gear, slid
this way and that, his garbled words
so unintelligible we cried.

If I leave this house, I'm not coming back.
And I said, *No, you will be back.*
And he said, *I don't want to leave.*
And I said, *You will be back.*
He stood for the last time, pulled his socks on
wrapped his Indian chief bathrobe tight,
padded across the lit lawn, circled
by neighbors, knowing what he knew.

Dead Rose

Disbelieving he would never move,
I rubbed his shirtfront, startled
at the wood hardness beneath
pressed cotton, a mannequin of a dad.
Before he left the room,
I removed his glasses
to slip them into his jacket pocket
where they sat most of the time.
My fingers emerged
scattering dry, papery, brown flecks
as I recovered the dead white rose
I pinned to his lapel eight months ago
when we danced at my cousin's wedding.

Salt Stings

The sky wears a Virgin Mary blue cape.
The aroma of aged bulkheads rife
with the salt of the Long Island Sound.
Layers of tar seam the splintering
planks, keep the cliff from tumbling
into the sand. The iodine smell
of dried seaweed, its briny taste,
a substance my father said we'd discover
would be worth eating—good for you,
as all things from the sea. I try
to recall the other secrets he told me
about life above and below the sea.

Just One Thing

for DF

Tremors of the head, eyes, hands,
the almost invisible hearing aid,
your swift pride to replace it.

Each week our writing group meets
at the long, slate table on chrome legs
firm on the Oriental rug with its own Moroccan story.

I stack dirty dishes, retreat into the kitchen.
You always cook too much for diners
who gush over the simplest recipes.

You join me, we roll our eyes.
Like our ancestors, we know where there is bread
there is life, unthinkable to be without it.

Now, with death in the room, we rearrange
line breaks, curse politicians,
sip wine after wine.

Bottles line up, empty jewels headed
for recycling plants, to be pulverized,
reappear transformed, unrecognizable.

You doze.

I linger.

I want the most permanent thing about you.
I want the black table.

Romance

I stand beneath
the Eiffel Tower's black steel netting
knowing my father's French past

kept him one step beyond
the surly brood of Italian men
filing into the parlor on Sundays.

A WWII vet, he taught the Senegalese, Algerians,
tutored me in an ethical landscape
of honor, loyalty—old-fashioned words.

He and his friends Yves, Viggo, Rolanda
never belied their resistance days,
ordinary heroics in a living room in Queens.

Signs

Your wife rushes
to her lawyer
about wills, trusts
to fortify herself
against greedy children.

With her bum leg
and cane, she makes it
to the car. The instant
she arrives, a pigeon
feather alights
on the windshield.

She takes short, nervous
breaths, overwrought
by the prospect
of hiring a lawyer or anyone.
*What do you think
daddy would think of this?*
I ask the feather,
Is that you, dad?
She looks sideways
at me like a pigeon
from the corner
of its eye, tsks,
*I don't know
if that's daddy.*

The feather travels
inside Dad's car beside
maps, water bottles,
sunglasses, his new gloves.

Wakes

Uncle Joe is flanked
by garish fans of gladiolas
in Neopolitan reds, Sicilian magenta.
My non-Italian sister-in-law
calls them "Italian flowers."

My mother's Manhattan cousins
a sub-tribe of the larger tribe—
huddle, live together, eat together,
never leave West 4th St., never marry.
One sneezes and they all catch cold.

Aunt Katie is serene
in her supporting role.
Her husband, Joe
lies in the satin-lined casket.

His old self stares out of photographs
set in fancy silver frames
in the funeral parlor.
He really did look like Valentino.

My aunt smiles to herself,
shakes her head and sighs,
Joe so loved himself.

I Listen

I see them in a heaven steaming with kitchen vapors.
Zi' Catuzza rolling her napkin into cigarillos
repeating her mantra, "No man is good enough for any woman."
She had a bad husband I tell myself.
Zia Raffaela presses vanilla *pizzelle*
Cugina Lisabetta beats an octopus into submission,
cooks it pink, sprinkled with olive oil, lemon, oregano.

I hear laughter among them, I am
on the other side of the curtains one of them sewed—
it matches the tablecloths, the aprons made
of remnants gathered from the sweatshop floor.
Forbidden to banter, I am invisible, but I see them.

Through the drone of mom's lunch report today,
"I heated up the salmon, my knees are talking
to me all day, so I stayed in, then I made myself
a nice cup of coffee…"
I want to moan, I tune her out, yet hear
Zi' Catuzza's other mantra, "You only get one mother…"

Mom says, "I had a busy night last night,
my room was full of visitors."
The march of the unrestful dead—husband, sisters, cousins.
She says, "My mother reminded me of the things
we used to make for Christmas.
Stuffed olives, pickled zucchini, eggplant salad…
you know how your grandmother was," I couldn't rest,
I snap to attention
scribble down the recipes.

III.

Lovestuck

I jog to the Borghese Gardens,
pass the zoo's furless creatures
bound up the steps
to Cardinal Scipione's Galleria,
catch a glimpse
of the Bernini sculptures
assuming their positions
on pedestals
in time to gape
at us studying them.
They've returned breathless
from a Bacchanalian feast,
careful not to stain
their marble bodies with blood rich wine.
I imagine Apollo rushing Daphne
who will never be caught
in her desire to stay pure and free.
Like nosey neighbors,
the sculptures follow the drama,
throw their heads back,
recall yesterday's spectators
peering up Apollo's crotch
wrapped by Daphne's fingers
metamorphosed into laurel leaves
that clutch the warmest part
of his smooth, marble body
staking her claim forever.

How ever did you know

which book I should bring on the flight?
How did you know which poems I'd love
want to read over and over?

My lips form the words,
my ears hear whispers
of phonetic harmony,
accents, my favorite vowels
while riding trains past
the Postojna Caves in snow,
lacy edges of the Adriatic.

How ever did you know
which words would kiss me
with each passing birch, willow.

Un Beso en Cuba—A Kiss in Cuba

Back with your right
forward with your left
Cross body turn—press her.
Let her know it's coming.
¡Ahora, enchufa!

Johnny Pacheco swings
a *ritmo cubano.*
Smutty studio windows
the wooden floor pale and
polished under dancing feet
stepping, pounding, turning.
A door slips open—
Cuban couple's feet
are loving the moment.

Let her foot get in the middle
your feet stay on the outside.
¡Ahora, una vuelta!

I look down at the pattern
un beso with his pelvis
his feet frame mine.
Can lesson one get
this sexy, this fast
in sultry Havana?

La Nebbia Veneziana—Fog in Venice

Robed and twice-twined
with the plush terry cloth robe
that came with my posh room,
I dress for the steaming pool
on this chilly winter night.

The first night of *Carnevale* in Venice
Beyond this mineral bath
children run among the shadows
with red capes, devils' horns,
men wear three-cornered hats
as they do in *Rigoletto*
and women press bulbous breasts
above lace bodices and jeweled skirts.

I can barely see the pool
the fog is so thick
the steam heady—the odor
of boiled eggs rising.

The fog never touches me,
never settles on any surface
swift as a breath,
steam without the fear of heat,
a mist that leaves shadows in the spotlight.

I part the steam with each movement.
It folds over me, behind me,
protects me from the cold night air,
from the light, from the eyes
of the other solitary swimmer.

I hear the water
part in lopsided movements.
Not synchronized,
but in jagged intervals.
He is passing me.
He is invisible.

I would like to ask him to swim in silence,
to make no waves in this temple of steam.

Birds on a Box

She takes all the risks
to share her dinner with him.
Dives under the river's surface
to retrieve enough for two.
Identical, interchangeable
after so much time spent
in each other's company.
A unit, an association,
a morality play about monogamy.
At twilight the river runs cool
with unexpected warm spots.
She repeats the rite: ducks,
swoops, lunges, emerges
with a morsel of pierced protein,
what is hers is his is hers.

Déjà vu

We promised each other never
to spend Christmas alone nor
would we ever eliminate
Christmas from our calendar
or our lives as we did in 1992.

It fell on a Sunday that year
and Rod Serling would be
introducing Twilight Zone
episodes for 24 hours,
shows I knew by heart.

We hardly spoke.
I moved the TV into the bedroom,
something I never thought I'd do,
but I needed a companion that day,
even the conundrums of freaks in a small box
quieted my nerves. I watched
Serling's bushy eyebrows curl
and crawl across his forehead
as he'd say: *Welcome to
the Twilight Zone, perhaps
you have been here before.*

Demons

Deep in sleep,
you coax my small demons away
they scamper into night's vapor.

Let me rest
to the low murmur of your voice
describing the beach at Luquillo
listening to small waves lapping
at low tide.

Your small, muscular hands slide
down and up and down my spine,
one vertebra at a time,
across the ribs
you would know anywhere in any dark.

A shaft of cool moonlight throws
the boyish curve of your man's face
into relief.

I breathe in your essence
in one long deep breath
to absorb your peace.

Just before sleep takes me
under the weight
of your solitary palm,
you cup the pulse I surrender.

Spring

> *after Kenneth Koch*
> *and Tracy K. Smith*

Let's not talk,
not a word
this morning.
There are so many
things to say
too many to start the day.
A light rain is falling
so faint it cannot be
seen or felt or heard.
Let's moan low into
winter's covers,
rub elbows, knees
let's write love songs.
Let's get silly
hop on a train into the city.
See commuters
strung up with palm pilots,
blackberrys, cell phones
hear sirens in spring
sway with the jolt of brakes.
Are you with me?
Let's not talk.

Let ourselves record
this moment we will
revisit again and again on
a cold, biting dark day
in January
when snow soaks our boots
flies in our eyes
we will have a spring morning memory
in an unremembered year.
For now, let's not talk
as we shake sleep
I mouth your name
have I told you
you are gorgeous in spring
trading the bulk of wool
for a day in the park,
a ride in the dark
sshh, let's not talk
I prefer to watch you
in spring,
shrug off winter
Don't say a word
travel in your dreams
arrive just for me.

When Magritte Wasn't Looking

When is an apple an apple?

When it is not a painting of an apple.

Or, when its high chartreuse makes us disbelieve its waxen sheen, and size, larger than the palace behind it.

It tells us something.

That, it is an apple overgrown, overcome with itself, so vast, it drowns all sense of time, emits a faint perfume from the skin still sealed tight.

Once the skin is pierced, diced, shared with someone you love, someone familiar with the ritual of slicing symmetrical crescents to be consumed without sharp cheddar cheese or peanut butter or dripping with melted chocolate marring its pulp and skin.

Compare this to a baked apple.

Its skin shriveling as sugar bubbles out of its core to gurgle and rise from its bulbous green body, trembling in the heat of a roasting pan, settling once it hits the cool air, its pulp ready to receive the spoon that scoops out its heart.

Bats

At night I dream of baby bats
flitting out of the kitchen molding.

Up a stepstool I climb,
fly swatter in hand
slip it deftly into the crevice
to ease one out.
The smallest bat skitters back in.
I step down to the linoleum floor.
The bat reappears, clinging
to the ceiling above me
quivering.

Pipistrello,
the Italian word for bat that sounds
like the sounds they make when they fly
in black formations over our heads
almost invisible, always audible.

I am relieved when you appear.
You look up,
silent, arrive at a solution.
Your steady hands,
solid shoulders
move through the air.
Gentle and swift,
you steer the bat to the window
let it fly out into the midnight sky.

IV.

Skippy

My family has had a long,
unsentimental history with pets.
Skippy was a spitz-collie,
a breed known for impatience,
rapid fire judgment, bad temper.
He belonged to my grandfather
but he was no pet.
Not to be toyed with, Skippy or *Shkeepe*
had a white widow's peak over his forehead
that deepened when he was about to snap.
Nonno walked *Shkeepe* on a tire chain leash
the handle anchored by a steel T
that fit squarely between his
third and fourth knobby fingers.
When he ducked into a store
for his contraband De Nobili cigars,
my grandfather tied Skippy's
leash to the bumper of a truck
that vanished up Sutphin Boulevard
to Jamaica without noticing the dog.
Skippy ran at top speed for miles
barking until he was released.
His raw and bloody paws bandaged,
the vet did not leave much hope.
When *Nonno* walked through the door,
Shkeepe stood up on all four paws
peed on the stainless steel table,
a sign of life if ever there was one.

A tavola!—Sit Down at the Table!

As soon as it is five o'clock
The diners take their assigned seats.

Nonna at the head of the table
My father at the foot—
balancing the seesaw of power.

My mother jumps up and down
Like a scared rabbit—
serving one ego at a time.

Jean, couldya sit down...
she could sit but a moment,
never swallowing a crumb.

With one long gesture, she spears
the largest veal cutlet,
sweeps it to my father's plate.

Nonna glares at her daughter
as she serves her husband first,
the man Nonna calls "strange blood."

Nonno is uninterested in the order of servings.
Sips a wine of his own making
from a free glass from the gas station.

He peers out from under a lock of thick white hair
To be sure the Vesuvius he calls a wife
is content—for the moment.

The little sisters' large olive eyes
decipher the seat of power
knowing it is a lesson to remember.

Lethal

"We're not short, we're petite,"
she'd say, "Good things come
in small packages."
"You don't want to be a lanky
glass of water, do you"?
My mother had an arm's length
of ways to shrink the diminutive
nicknames: shorty, short stack,
adorable, peanut, inch, midge, runt.
At five-foot nothing,
I wanted to be, if not average,
then at least five foot two
like Gidget, Natalie Wood.

Ballet lengthened my spine,
though I took up little space
in the studio. Short meant
I was first in line, in the front row.
I learned not to waste motion,
stayed close to the core,
my center of gravity.
To balance *en pointe,*
spin double *pirouettes,*
coil on occasion,
lethal, small and ready to spring.

Marble King

My grandmother's broad figure
fills the doorway of 150-22 116th Drive.
Looming large at the top of the
red brick stoop in Jamaica, Queens,
she is a force rather than
a body of grand proportions,
the protector of territory and tradition.

In the shadow behind that door
is a round tin cache of glass marbles,
jewels of street games.
Hundreds of them gleam
from the dark corner—tiger eyes, cats' eyes,
flamingo pinks, royal and sky blues,
lime greens. On hot summer nights
we use the tin as a doorstop.

If my grandmother is the guard,
my brother is the prince.
Only his brown square fingers could
fondle, flip, skip, let the marbles
clink softly, he practiced daily.
I study the flash of rolling colors
loll across the wood-planked floor.

He stores his favorites in a chamois sack
in his front pockets. When he moves,
I hear the muffled sounds
from across the room,
chink, chink in folds of fabric.
Envision them eyeballing
each other in the dark,
winking at me.

Imagine filling the palms of my hands
with the cool spheres, rolling
a cold glass marble between my fingers
letting it roll ever so gently over my tongue.

Cornrows

Cheryl's cornrows crisscross
her round head that tops
her dark, Trinidadian neck.

Her mother jelly-coats
her coffee-colored fingers to move
rapid and sure through nappy, crinkled hair.

She pulls one rope of hair
over the other, over the other,
over the other, until
the braids are locked down tight
with barrettes, ribbons and bows.

Around the corner at Jean's Beauty Parlor
white women plop into wide leather chairs
as metallic chemicals crimp and whip
their soft hair into prim tootsie roll curls.

Across the street Sylvia's is crammed
arm to shiny bronze arm with black women
pressing their hair—make it straight, straight,
shiny, smooth as seals—take the nap out.

Cheryl and I watch Angela Davis,
who never lived in Queens,
the land of smooth and straight,
cry out of the TV.

She raises her fist past a brazen halo
of naturally kinky hair
letting her 'fro fly loud and free,
as if her hair said, *I will not hide,
I am trouble, see me now.*

Cheryl's cornrows, a puzzle of braids
locked down tight, tight, tight.
I run my fingers along the satin rope
down my spine—wishing all the while
best friends could look more alike.

Inside

Hermes' legs and wings flash
on the pinewood bookshelf.
Rows of hard-won trophies lined up
in order of height.

When you were not home, I would slip
into your room of somber browns
with knick-knacks and trophies.

A halo of dust gathered at the base
of each pedestal—some of marble,
others metal or plastic.

I moved with care
among your museum pieces, arranged
to catch an invasive sibling or a thief.

If I shifted a trophy even a centimeter,
I'd replace it so you would not
notice the altered dust patterns.

A careless sleeve could give me away,
wiping the dust could create a crescent shape.

As if challenged to tread
in forbidden territory spiced with Canoe and soap,
I would lie on your bed,
listen to your records—Joan Baez, the Weavers.

Not satisfied with touring your room,
sometimes I borrowed items,
a belt once hid for years in my closet.

Backing out of the room,
I double-checked all was in place,
no new creases on the bed, no dust puffs altered,
careful not to leave my scent behind.

Thieves in the Family

Cousin Tony says "nigger"
every chance he gets,
a wise guy, he
raves and rants.

Didn't anyone ever tell him
that in his mother's country
Sicilians are the Ns?

Apart from the N-word, Tony is ok.
He built a wooden dollhouse for his daughter,
carved pint-sized people and miniature furniture
not covered with plastic.

He joined the *Sons of Italy* to get
his traffic tickets fixed,
still, he robbed my grandmother's
Chinese bulbs during her funeral.

My ninety-year old mother still mourns
the loss of those bulbs. She retaliates.
Pilfers basil, parsley, tomatoes
from his garden, growing
next to grandmother's Chinese lilies,

furtive, filling her lungs with the flowers' scent.

Before It Gets Tough

Standing on my father's feet
we waltzed in the kitchen
waiting for the dough
to rise—punch it down
two times, spin and dip
flour on our faces
yeast in our breaths.

We talked about my future
as actress, teacher,
lawyer, nun, writer.
I said I would write short
stories, long poems.
He said, *Will you write
about me?* Of course.

My mother would pop her head in
roll her eyes as she surveyed
the kitchen counters
piled high with bowls,
spoons covered with elastic dough.

He once worked on a dairy farm
in Walkill, supplied
West Point cadets with milk.
The stainless steel
milking machines
shocked the cows,
made them cranky.
He went back to the old way
of squeezing their teats, petting
their behinds.

Like cows, the dough must be kneaded
just right. Don't overhandle
or you lose the lightness,
make it heavy, grainy. Stop
before it gets tough.

Brother

One of three girls, I share my room.
I wonder if you ever get lonely
in your own room in a house of great sounds
and milling relatives ignoring the bounds
of thresholds and doors.

Apart from parents, grandparents, sisters, pets,
you'd lie at night in the coolest room in summer
and winter, the shady corner of the house,
the sun never splashes across your bedspread
as it does mine each morning.

Whenever I look at your door, it is closed.

We must have known

it was mostly hopeless,
yet each day I drove
past wide open gates
and green lawns,
dropped off your listless
body at the curb.
Watched you
in the rearview mirror,
stooped and crumbling.
You'd wait for me.
We followed
the motions, greeted
the nurses, the doctors
as if we believed
there was a way out.
Your back to me,
I watched your reflection
through the window,
fluorescent lights
etched creases beneath
high cheekbones,
eyes that sparked until
you were gothic
and lucent.

The Call

A fall from
a three-story roof,
not a big building,
serious enough
to break bones.
A day later,
another call.
A room
at Jacobi Hospital.

I plan.
He drives.
She'll be there, you know.
I know,
the mother is
always there.

The cycle—failure,
salvation, failure,
passive,
remote control.
Lateral moves
ward to ward.
Suicide watch.

The mother takes him back.
He doesn't get better.
He never leaves
except this way.

I watch
from the perimeter,
Stepmother
not blood, not natural.

Despair respects no borders
legal, illegal.
You love what
you touch, love more
what touches you.

Empty Chairs

*In the name of the father
and of the son,* but what of
the daughters, sisters, mothers?

It's an Italian woman's trick
to look just so, ears sealed.

Like a bitter clerk
you tally your inventory of grievances.

Your discontent starts
with the women of this house.

Over veal cutlets and salad,
biscotti, espresso,
wine from the cellar.

Our father no longer speaks,
crawls from bed to table
to couch, eyes and ears alert.

Orphan, farmer, father,
You nail him for his biggest crime—
failing to measure success in dollars.

Your chilling condemnations
insipid, duplicitous, vain—
echo on the cold enamel kitchen table.

We are the serfs who dance
to the beat of our father's pain,

Take notes when doctors lie,
wash fecal-spattered sheets,
count the place settings,
remove the empty chairs.

Bleach y *chorizos*

Found myself at "our" place
China/Latina, our days, nights
at St. Vincent's trying to find
a refuge for the runaway,
your child, my stepson,
half Puerto Rican, half Italian.

Comfort in the wafts of
bleach and chorizos served
by Spanish-speaking Chinese men
pencil slim in shiny black slacks
white shirts, black bowties
a hint of Aqua Velva.

The musty odor greets you
as if you are visiting your
grandmother. The scent is
thick as dark green linoleum
café con leche spumes
from Chinese men with Latin hearts.

The Boys

The last time the boys visited
I prepared their favorite dishes
trusting in aromatic memories to quell

the jitters—theirs and mine.
One just out of jail,
the other from a mental hospital.

Wash your hands,
no hats at the table—
kufi, or baseball caps.

One quoted the Koran,
the other, the Bible and Malcolm X.

They argued over an eye for an eye
Louis Farrakhan, Jesus, Gandhi
'til the table held
more guests and then more.

After *ziti, cacciatore,*
salad and coffee, I took
old photo albums out

to remind them who they were,
who they are.

V.

Mantras

She went to India to memorize
to study on bended knee, head bowed
to utter *om*
Follow her breath rise fall
through the fine cilia
that line her nostrils
departing at the count of eight.
Hushed whisper travels well
from nose to mouth and back.
Not unlike repeating the rosary
fingers following the chained circle
one bead at a time.

Sparrow Hawks

They call us sparrow hawks,
the smallest birds of prey
at ten inches. They prefer open spaces.
The human variety deviates.
Work in crowded urban centers,
find solace in anonymity yet remain
visible as hostesses or stewardesses
in hotels, on ships, airplanes.

These falcon family birds hover
above intended prey,
which is smaller still
birds, spiders, reptiles, grasshoppers,
crickets, mice, caterpillars.

Western women pity us, our
men scorn us, and our sisters
fear for us, the veil, illiteracy,
genital mutilation, we seem
hopeless, backward, astray.

Men call them
sparrow hawks of neocolonialism,
women who have unnaturally
used their energies for materialism,
instead of as "god" intended.

Chetty's Cats

Feline refugees of Palermo's cesspool puddles
leap through open windows
saunter past jasmine-scented doorjambs
in the white, noon light.

At mealtimes,
take their places at her feet.
Cousins refuse to dine with her,
but the cats are prompt.
The black one looks as if someone
has ironed her ribs exposing raw pink flesh
the gray one has one eye
the other's ear is but a comma.

Mad with Fear

She stands alone atop a bleached white
fortress overlooking the turquoise Adriatic.
The dry *bura* wind brushes
the heat of spring's sun over her skin
a wind only nature could invent
and usually saves for winter.

Franiça moved to Dubrovnik's old city
protected by tall, thick limestone walls.
Not for a moment did we think
they would bomb the Old Town
not Napoleon, not Hitler did such a thing.

Even when the bombs fell in the "shelling hours,"
We slept sometimes for sixteen hours a day.
I have never slept so many hours.
So much of my life…just spent sleeping.
Sometimes when we woke
we could not hear, we could not speak.

Her pale, wide-spaced eyes
sag at the outer corners.
I wonder if they looked that way
before the war, before the shelling,
before the long sleeps,
before sharing five liters
of water each day among so many
who needed to drink or bathe.

At night we tied our wrists one to another
so we could not be lost,
her head lifts, eyes lock on mine for the first time.
And we laughed for no reason. Mad with fear.

Just Boys

The sun is about to slip below the grass,
below the stones. 1400 identical tombs
lining the heart of San Donato,
the Allied cemetery in Abruzzo.
I step before one granite slab
to another, reading their names
out loud, as soon as I read
them, I forget. Annoyed with myself
I snap photos as if a camera could
capture silence. I calculate their ages
to bring them to life. Three
tombstones are set aside. Three
German names, three
boys who fought the other boys.
Boys resting in the same place,
sharing the same view of the Adriatic.

Illegal

We are somebody
and we are from somewhere.
They camp at the airport,
on the tarmac, the Libyans step on them,
beat them, whipping dogs.

They call them *abd,* slaves.
Darker than all the rest,
lower than the Chinese
working in Libya for years.
They are trapped.

Tell someone, we are dying.

Autumn in the Algarve

Cherry-faced
Brits, Germans
with crooked teeth,
fast smiles,
bellies bounce in buggies
over and under Algarve
golf courses
off season, half-price.
Breakfast tables
piled high with croissants,
rolls, Portuguese tortillas
under a canopy facing
the Atlantic rolling
to the sounds of Cape Verde,
dining on coffee from Angola,
shrimp from Mozambique,
courtesy of Portugal's
children disguised
as butlers and maids.

Missive from the Sunny Southwest

for Ron Butler

They're already calling it the *Al Gore
Global Warming Snowstorm.*
Snow everywhere in Arizona
with three-foot drifts piled
up against the door. How
am I going to get out?
Here at the Camino Real they're asking
for volunteers to push the wheelchair bound.
The big transports are supposed
to be dropping food supplies.
The dryers in the laundry room
are frozen solid. Ghostly vapors
rise from the pool. My main concern:
cabin fever. Send money.

Hunger

After Dina's husband left her
the white walls seemed drab,
invisible on some days. She
painted the kitchen lemon,
the living room peach,
the dining room asparagus,
her bedroom, watermelon.
Her mother-in-law thought
it was her Italian heritage,
her ex-husband thought
she was hungry.

VI.

Goes Silent

for CK

My mother and I knew
not to disturb the nest
If you get too close,
the mother will abandon them.

The three-year-old boy munches
corn-colored cereal bits,
stares above at the twigs,
dry grass slipping out of the nest
the sparrows built inside a coffee can.

The boy's eyes do not leave
the nest. Sits cross-legged,
wide-eared for peeps from the can.

The nest goes silent.
The boy waits for the birds to fly.

Small Victories

Your mother loved words
Sent you to learn "real" Italian
to forget the staccato Calabrese
iddu, idda, ghista, ghistu.
You cocked your ears
to other dialects, studied Dante.

She wanted you
to become *a type-a-writer.*
You rebelled, wanted
to work with your hands.
Sketched haute couture designs
from window displays.
Cut and sewn from remnants
your cousin smuggled
from sweatshops.
Stayed up all night
creating head-to-toe ensembles.

A bonbon of a hat added
inches to your small frame.
Your white polka dot dress
billowed at the sleeves,
a heart-shaped neck dipped toward
a hip-hugging skirt over curves,
delirious with the victories your hands
promised and delivered in the night.

Named for Royalty

for Mafalda and Jennie

My mother named me
Mafalda Yolanda Margherita
after all the King's daughters. I just hated it.
There I was, sewing buttons on cardboard squares,
forty cents for 144 and named for royalty.
I remember the shop I went to for my first job.
It was down some steps on South St., like a dungeon.
All the girls at the machines were wearing
their underwear and skimpy blouses. I was so proud
of my diploma, how smart I was,
but all the floor man wanted
was to see me in my underwear.

C'era una volta—Once Upon a Time

Snow White travels
with Seven Dwarves in tow.
Could it mean that women get
seven little men to serve them? Or,
did they stand for the seven deadly sins?
Cinderella or *Cenerentola,* the abused bastard
of a houseful of spiteful hens,
came close behind, followed
by Red Riding Hood, Rapunzel,
pale blondes who tossed
their hair out windows or wore
braids wrapped like little crowns.

I knew them for what they were,
"paper dollies," no one would want
to resemble for more than a minute
because they'd blow away.
Instead, I sat unnoticed among
the *vecchietti,* the elders on Saturday mornings
to watch Continental Miniatures'
black and white edgy heroines
like the wild-eyed Anna Magnani,
sweaty, bloody, hair as black as crows
and opera as common as the tar on streets.

Unlike my friends' American parents,
Italian *nonni* never sheltered me
from impassioned tales of fallen women.
Mamma Roma's midriff rolled
through cheap black satin
as Magnani fended off tricks
on her pilgrimage
to right her life, sell fresh fruit,
win her son back, fly
into the snare of madness,
in a dialect I always understood.

Coming Up for Air

The soap smell of lilacs brushes past me today
as it did so many times swimming
in the little rubber pool behind your house.

Four eyes watched me, as I stayed
in close earshot of the secret whispers
between sisters. Raised my chin to watch
my mother place icepacks
on the purple stains that circled your eye.

I ducked underwater blowing bubbles
dog paddled my way along the bottom
feeling the bumpy earth beneath,
coming up to breathe in the lilacs.

Away

Seven-year-old me basks
in the moment—
I am the only child tagging
along with you, holding hands
on a quiet street where there are
no cars, no traffic lights,
no dogs or people—just us.

We were going to visit someone
who, I can't remember.
It may have been spring
as we walked without coats
swinging our arms in synch.

You carry a gift bag
We are both happy
to be away from home.
Out of the sight of your mother,
my grandmother

whose limitless scolding
up the stairs to our three-room
apartment shared by six
has you trembling
each time she summons
you to the top of the stairs.

You are saved by the steps
she cannot climb.
For her, it is enemy territory
inhabited by you, your children
and the man you married,
the eternal outsider.

You are smiling and going
away from the house.
We're holding hands under the sun
on our way to a place I cannot name.

Amore on Hope Street

My mother-in-law and I
swivel into wooden captain's chairs
at Amore's on Hope St.
The music is low but audible,
Frank Sinatra sings *The Lady is a Tramp.*
I guess they like Frank Sinatra.
    Why do you say that? she asks.
Because they play him every time we come here.
    Oh, is it playing now?
Yes, but low,
not to bring attention
to her diminished hearing.
    I was thinking a lot about him a few days ago.
Really, what made you think of him?
Knowing she boycotted Sinatra
for his bad politics, his mob ties.
Well, you mentioned he was singing, you know.
She catches me in a web of warped time.
Louie Prima and Keely Smith croon
through the *rollatini.*
We make it to espresso
sipping to Connie Francis'
holy hymn of "Mamma."
My mother-in-law looks up.
    Did Frank Sinatra die?
I want to burst out laughing
at the silly, senseless exchange,
the same question each time we meet.
Yes, he died,
The corners of her mouth turn down,
she leans back, shoulders droop.
but not so long ago,

I kick myself for not lying.
> *I was always very fond of him.*
> *Did he mean a lot to you?*
> *Well, yes, he did,* as if recalling an old love affair.
> *Do you know how old I am?*
> Yes, I do.
> *I can't believe how old I am.*

Afraid

At 85, Jennie is scared
of everything
won't dial the doctor,
won't write a will, but
takes a flight to California

for Easter, the
Resurrection
on the west coast
where traditionally,
the sun goes down.

Ladies who lunch

at Le Bernardín prefer oysters
no larger than two inches.
Briny, muscular, manageable,
the most popular are widow's holes,
like a punch line to a dirty joke
about the world's favorite aphrodisiac.
Instead, it is named for a widow
married to a lost-at-sea whaler
who lived on the Peconic
where oysters are born, bred,
cultivated to lady-like taste.
If left alone, can live for fifteen years,
grow to foot-long sea creatures.
Almost inert, inanimate as a plant,
oysters live sealed inside shells,
filled with their own juice.
Take one firm bite
or the creature will live on
in your stomach, say the French.
Puff your cheek with its liquor,
taste the salty air, a sweet creature.
Slurp, never chew. Tease it,
work it with your tongue,
never sink your teeth in, goodness no.
Yet others say, *If you swallow,*
all oysters are the same.

Longing

A din of voices, rattling dishes, clinking silverware
I keep him at my table longer than I should

To rendezvous with black eyes, black ringlets, a nose
that grows over a dazzling, generous mouth...

All about to vanish in the dusty, scattered mind
of a 50-something woman with a dab
of longing behind each ear lobe.

Comfort Zone

She shadows people's sounds
in bars, restaurants,
charts their courses
across crowded rooms.

Peopled subway cars, a mine
of foreign bodies violating
the eighteen-inch comfort zone,
flesh pressed against flesh,
against steel, poles protect.
Conversations spoken nose to nose
erupt and simmer.

She sneaks up behind them
a Mata Hari of the spoken word.
Non-sequiturs seep into her pen,
appear on her pages,
compel her to scribble,
stealing strangers' whispers.

She revisits her notebooks
to discover a germ,
a word that sings or rises or claps
or makes a striking sound
leaping off the page in surprise or ecstasy.

So many trail like mouse droppings
leading nowhere, to be swept away
in favor of more perfect moments
that may one day
sit cross-legged on a tightrope
like smiling acrobats in the sun.

My Rain

does not whip the ground
from under me.

Falls straight
     as a sheet.

Ends at dawn
   in a mist that lingers
   over blades of grass.

photo by Nancy Ruhling

Maria Lisella's work appears in *Amore on Hope Street* (Finishing Line Press) and *Two Naked Feet* (Poets Wear Prada). Her poetry has appeared in many literary journals in print and online including *Fox Chase Review, Liqueur 44* (France), *New Verse News, The New York Quarterly, The Paterson Literary Review,* and *Skidrow Penthouse.*

She is the co-curator for the Italian American Writers Association readings at Cornelia St. Café and Sidewalk Café. She lives in Long Island City with her husband Gil Fagiani, a poet, translator and writer.

Lisella is a writer and editor covering the travel industry and Europe for more than 20 years. Born in Queens, New York, she graduated from The City Univeristy of New York's Queensborough Community College, Queens College, and holds an M.A. in Specialized Journalism from NYU-Polytechnic University. She has taught non-fiction writing, and currently teaches a course in Tourism and Hospitality at the Borough of Manhattan Community College.

Her travel writing appears online and in print in a wide array of publications including *FOXNews.com, AFAR, Travel and Leisure, the New York Daily News, Star Ledger,* and others. She has been recognized for her work on Italy, South Africa, and France.

The New York Quarterly Foundation, Inc.
New York, New York

Poetry Magazine

Since 1969

Edgy, fresh, groundbreaking, eclectic—voices from all walks of life.

Definitely NOT your mama's poetry magazine!

The *New York Quarterly* has been defining the term contemporary American poetry since its first craft interview with W. H. Auden.

Interviews • Essays • and of course, lots of poems.

www.nyq.org

No contest! That's correct, NYQ Books are NO CONTEST to other small presses because we do not support ourselves through contests. Our books are carefully selected by invitation only, so you know that NYQ Books are produced with the same editorial integrity as the magazine that has brought you the most eclectic contemporary American poetry since 1969.

Books

www.nyq.org

poetry at the edge™

www.ingramcontent.com/pod-product-compliance
Lightning Source LLC
LaVergne TN
LVHW041341080426
835512LV00006B/561